# URVASHI

URVASHI, THE PEERLESS CELESTIAL DANCER, WAS THE FAVOURITE OF INDRA. ONCE, AFTER DANCING IN THE HALLS OF KUBERA, SHE WAS RETURNING HOME ACCOMPANIED BY A FEW OTHER APSARAS.

SUDDENLY—

THE ASURAS CARRIED OFF URVASHI AND HER CLOSE COMPANION, CHITRALEKHA.

HELP!

HELP!

JUST THEN KING PURURAVAS, A FRIEND OF KING INDRA, PASSED BY IN HIS CHARIOT.

DEAR APSARAS, YOU LOOK TERRIFIED. WHO HAS DARED TO HARM YOU?

NOT US...OUR FRIENDS..... URVASHI AND CHITRALEKHA.... THE ASURAS HAVE KIDNAPPED THEM.

DO NOT WORRY. I WILL RESCUE THEM. WAIT FOR ME ON YONDER HILL-TOP.

PURURAVAS RODE OFF ON HIS MISSION.

AFTER A WHILE—

AH! REJOICE! THERE...KING PURURAVAS WITH OUR FRIENDS...

IN THE CHARIOT—

URVASHI, OPEN YOUR EYES. YOU ARE AN APSARA MAIDEN. SUCH TERROR DOES NOT BECOME YOU!

THE ASURAS HAVE BEEN OVERCOME.

BY WHOM? WAS IT INDRA WHO....

IT WAS PURURAVAS, THE MIGHTY. EVEN INDRA HAS SOUGHT HIS AID WHEN HARD-PRESSED IN BATTLE.

URVASHI LOOKED UP AND HER EYES MET THOSE OF PURURAVAS.

WHAT A NOBLE MAN! THE ASURAS HAVE DONE ME A FAVOUR.

NEVER HAVE I BEHELD SUCH BEAUTY!

SUDDENLY URVASHI REMEMBERED HER COMPANIONS.

OUR FRIENDS? ARE THEY SAFE?

YES, THERE THEY ARE. CAN YOU SEE THEM ON THAT PEAK WAITING TO RECEIVE YOU?

AS SOON AS THE CHARIOT TOUCHED EARTH—

PURURAVAS THEN ENTRUSTED THE BEVY OF APSARAS TO THE CARE OF A GANDHARVA.

TAKE THEM SAFELY BACK TO MY FRIEND.

AS THE GANDHARVA'S CHARIOT SOARED INTO THE SKY—

MY NOBLE KING, WILL I EVER SEE YOU AGAIN?

SWEET URVASHI, HAVING STOLEN MY HEART YOU ARE TAKING MY VERY BEING WITH YOU.

PURURAVAS RETURNED TO HIS PALACE AT PRATISH-THANA. BUT NOT FOR A MOMENT COULD HE TAKE HIS MIND OFF URVASHI. HE BECAME MOODY AND MOROSE.

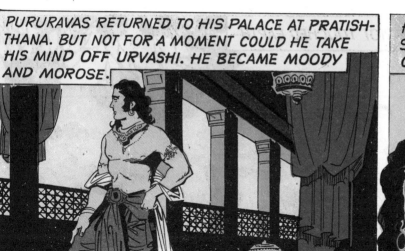

HIS FRIEND AND ADVISER, MANAVAKA, WAS CURIOUS.

WHAT AILS YOU, SIR?

PURURAVAS TOLD MANAVAKA ALL.

...AND NOW I AM SICK WITH LONGING FOR THE BEAUTIFUL APSARA.

YOUR QUEEN AWAITS YOUR PLEASURE. WHY DON'T YOU GO AND SEE HER?

PURURAVAS FELT GUILTY. HE HAD NOT SEEN HIS WIFE AUSHINARI SINCE HIS RETURN. HE HASTENED TO HER SIDE.

WELCOME, MY LORD! DID YOU MEET INDRA? DO THE ASURAS STILL TROUBLE HIM?

DEAR URVASHI, ALL WENT WELL. DO WAIT FOR ME TILL I FINISH SOME URGENT MATTERS OF STATE.

AND PURURAVAS LEFT.

7

MANAVAKA MEANWHILE WAS IN AGONY.

HIS SECRET WEIGHS HEAVILY ON ME. I'D BETTER KEEP AWAY FROM PEOPLE LEST I BLURT IT OUT. I'LL WAIT HERE FOR HIM.

NIPUNIKA TRACKED HIM DOWN AS HE SAT WORRYING ABOUT KEEPING THE SECRET.

NOBLE SIR. THE QUEEN IS HEART-BROKEN AND CANNOT BE CONSOLED.

WHY? HAS MY FRIEND OFFENDED HER IN ANY WAY?

IT SEEMS HE ADDRESSED HER BY THE NAME OF THAT WOMAN FOR WHOM HE IS PINING

WHAT! HE CALLED HER URVASHI?

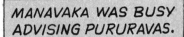
MANAVAKA WAS BUSY ADVISING PURURAVAS.

THERE ARE TWO WAYS OF KEEPING YOUR DIFFICULT MISTRESS WITH YOU FOREVER.

URVASHI'S HEART SANK WHEN SHE HEARD THAT.

OH! WRETCHED ME. HE LOVES ANOTHER.

WHY! YOU GIVE IN TO JEALOUSY LIKE A MORTAL WOMAN. WE ARE CELESTIALS, REMEMBER. LISTEN FURTHER.

MANAVAKA MEANWHILE WENT ON WITH HIS ADVICE.

EITHER SLEEP AS MUCH AS YOU CAN, SO YOU DREAM OF HER, OR PAINT URVASHI'S PORTRAIT AND GAZE AT IT.

BOTH IMPOSSIBLE.

WHY?

MY YEARNING WILL NOT LET ME SLEEP; AND MY TEARS WILL BLIND ME BEFORE THE PORTRAIT IS HALF FINISHED.

OH! IF ONLY SHE KNEW HOW I SUFFERED. PERHAPS SHE DOES AND YET CHOOSES TO BE CRUEL.

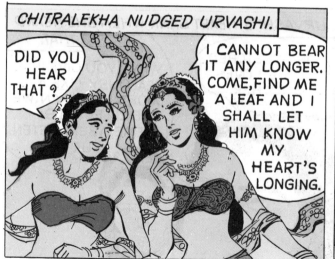

CHITRALEKHA NUDGED URVASHI.

DID YOU HEAR THAT?

I CANNOT BEAR IT ANY LONGER. COME, FIND ME A LEAF AND I SHALL LET HIM KNOW MY HEART'S LONGING.

CHITRALEKHA BROUGHT HER THE LEAF AND URVASHI WROTE HER MESSAGE ON IT.

PURURAVAS AND MANAVAKA STARTED IN SURPRISE AS THE LEAF FELL BETWEEN THEM.

A LEAF? WITH WRITING?

PERHAPS SHE HEARD YOUR LAMENT AND HAS ANSWERED.

PURURAVAS READ IT AND HIS FACE LIT UP WITH JOY.

YOU ARE RIGHT. IT IS A DECLARATION OF HER LOVE.

YOU ARE CONTENT NOW, I HOPE.

PLEASE HOLD THE LEAF. MY CLUMSY HANDS MIGHT ERASE THE SWEET LETTERS.

BUT WHY DOESN'T YOUR MISTRESS SHOW HERSELF?

AT THAT MOMENT CHITRALEKHA AND URVASHI REVEALED THEMSELVES.

URVASHI! I AM THE MOST FORTUNATE MAN ON EARTH. I HAVE WON YOUR LOVE.

JUST AS PURURAVAS TOOK HER HANDS IN HIS, A MESSENGER FROM THE COURT OF INDRA STOOD BEFORE THEM.

CHITRALEKHA! URVASHI! HURRY. INDRA AWAITS YOU. HE WANTS YOU TO DANCE LAXMI'S CHOICE FOR HIM.

AS URVASHI WENT—

I MUST NOT DETAIN YOU WHEN INDRA HIMSELF HAS SENT FOR YOU. BUT THINK OF ME SOMETIMES.

I SHALL— ALWAYS.

SHE IS GONE. OF WHAT USE ARE MY EYES TO ME NOW? AH! THE LETTER. WHERE IS MY LEAF?

WHAT?... OH!... THE LEAF. IT IS GONE. IT MUST HAVE FLOWN AFTER URVASHI.

13

BUT AUSHINARI WAS HAUGHTY AND COLD.

I AM SORRY FOR FORCING MY UNWELCOME PRESENCE ON YOU.

SHE TURNED TO GO AWAY.

DEAR QUEEN, I'M GUILTY. PLEASE FORGIVE ME.

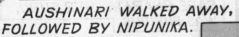

AUSHINARI WALKED AWAY, FOLLOWED BY NIPUNIKA.

AUSHINARI WAS IN TWO MINDS.

I SHOULD NOT BE WEAK-MINDED AND ACCEPT HIS HOLLOW APOLOGY. YET I CANNOT BEAR TO HURT HIM. BUT, NO....

WELL, SHE HAS REASON TO SPURN ME. THOUGH I LOVE URVASHI, I AM FOND OF HER TOO, AND HATE TO HURT HER. I WILL WAIT PATIENTLY TILL HER ANGER HAS COOLED DOWN.

15

MEANWHILE IN INDRA'S COURT, URVASHI'S DANCE WAS ON.

URVASHI PLAYED THE PART OF LAXMI. AS THE DANCE PROGRESS-ED —

OF ALL THE GODS ASSEMBLED HERE, TO WHOM DOES YOUR HEART BELONG?

PURURAVAS!

THE LOVE-STRUCK URVASHI HAD UTTERED THE NAME OF HER BELOVED INSTEAD OF REPLYING "PURUSHOTTAM." SAGE BHARATA, HER GURU, WAS FURIOUS.

YOU HAVE PUT ME TO SHAME! I BANISH YOU FROM HEAVEN.

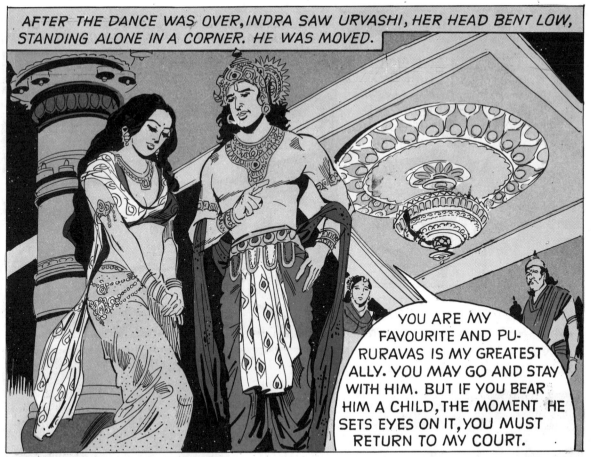

AFTER THE DANCE WAS OVER, INDRA SAW URVASHI, HER HEAD BENT LOW, STANDING ALONE IN A CORNER. HE WAS MOVED.

YOU ARE MY FAVOURITE AND PURURAVAS IS MY GREATEST ALLY. YOU MAY GO AND STAY WITH HIM. BUT IF YOU BEAR HIM A CHILD, THE MOMENT HE SETS EYES ON IT, YOU MUST RETURN TO MY COURT.

MEANWHILE AT PRATISHTHANA, QUEEN AUSHINARI REPENTED OF HER TREATMENT OF HER HUSBAND.

GO AND TELL YOUR MASTER, THE KING, THAT I AWAIT HIM TONIGHT ON THE TERRACE. I NEED HIS PRESENCE FOR A VOW I INTEND TAKING.

17

WHEN THE MESSAGE WAS GIVEN—

I SHALL CERTAINLY COME. I HAVE ALWAYS RESPECTED THE QUEEN'S WISHES.

PURURAVAS AND MANAVAKA ARRIVED ON THE TERRACE BEFORE THE APPOINTED HOUR.

LET US WAIT HERE FOR MY QUEEN.

AT THAT VERY MOMENT THE BANISHED URVASHI ACCOMPANIED BY CHITRALEKHA WAS ON HER WAY TO PURURAVAS.

LOOK! THERE HE IS ALONE WITH HIS FRIEND. LET US APPROACH HIM AND SHOW OURSELVES.

AS THEY WERE ABOUT TO PRESENT THEMSELVES TO PURURAVAS—

BUT THE QUEEN IS HERE.

BE CALM. THE QUEEN SEEMS DRESSED FOR SOME RITUAL. SHE WILL NOT STAY LONG. LET'S WATCH.

THE QUEEN ADVANCED.

MY HUSBAND!

WELCOME, MY QUEEN.

AUSHINARI'S REGAL BEARING AND EXQUISITE BEAUTY IMPRESSED URVASHI.

SHE IS MAJESTIC!

URVASHI'S SOUL IS PURE AND LOFTY. I'M PROUD OF HER.

AUSHINARI THEN TOOK HER VOW.

I, AUSHINARI, CALL UPON HEAVEN TO WITNESS MY VOW. I SHALL CLEANSE MY HEART OF JEALOUSY. HENCEFORTH I WILL WELCOME AS MY SISTER WHICHEVER WOMAN MY HUSBAND CHOOSES TO LOVE.

PURURAVAS WAS OVERWHELMED.

DEAR QUEEN! THIS VOW IS NOT NECESSARY. I AM NOT LOST TO YOU.

I HAVE TAKEN MY VOW.

SHE TURNED TO HER MAIDS.

LET US GO.

WAIT! DEAR ONE! DON'T LEAVE ME YET.

URVASHI WAS PUZZLED.

I DON'T UNDERSTAND ALL THAT IS GOING ON. BUT HER WORDS MAKE ME FEEL PURE AND FULL OF CONFIDENCE. I KNOW HE LOVES HIS WIFE AND YET I CANNOT BEAR TO GIVE HIM UP.

SHE'S GONE. OH! I WISH MY URVASHI WERE HERE NOW.

URVASHI WAS FILLED WITH A NEW BOLDNESS. SHE MADE HERSELF VISIBLE.

MY LORD! THE QUEEN HAS GIVEN YOU TO ME. I CAN NOW DARE TO LOVE YOU WITH ALL MY HEART AND BODY.

YOU ACCEPT ME BECAUSE MY QUEEN GAVE YOU PERMISSION. WHO PERMITTED YOU TO STEAL MY HEART?

URVASHI WAS TOO BASHFUL TO ANSWER HIM.

COME LET US GO TO THE GANDHA-MADANA GARDENS.

URVASHI AND PURURAVAS SPENT MANY HAPPY SEASONS IN GANDHAMA-DANA.

ONE DAY PURURAVAS SAW A BEAUTIFUL GIRL BY THE BANK OF A RIVER AND GAZED LONG AT HER.

URVASHI WAS SUDDENLY SEIZED WITH A FIT OF JEALOUS ANGER.

MY LORD IS CHARMED BY ANOTHER. HE NO LONGER LOVES ME !

SHE TURNED UPON HIM IN ANGER.

YOU ARE WELCOME TO JOIN HER. I'M GOING.

URVASHI ! WAIT ! BE REASON-ABLE.

BUT PUSHING HIM ASIDE, URVASHI RUSHED INTO A GROVE NEARBY.

SUDDENLY—

ALAS! ALAS! IN MY HASTE I'VE ENTERED THE WAR-LORD'S FORBIDDEN GROVE. O MY LORD! SAVE ME....

THE GROVE BELONGED TO KARTIKEYA, THE WAR-LORD AND WOMEN WERE FORBIDDEN FROM ENTERING IT. IF THEY DID, THEY WERE STRAIGHTAWAY TURNED INTO CREEPERS.

BUT ALL WAS NOT LOST. THERE WAS A WAY OUT, FOR KARTIKEYA HAD SAID—

IF A JEWEL FORMED OUT OF THE CRIMSON DYE DRIPPING FROM MY MOTHER'S FEET, TOUCHES THE WOMAN-TURNED-CREEPER, SHE WILL REGAIN HER OLD FORM.

PURURAVAS MEANWHILE SEARCHED IN VAIN FOR URVASHI. HE WANDERED AS ONE MAD, FOR SEVERAL DAYS, APPEALING TO ALL OF NATURE TO HELP HIM FIND HIS LOST LOVE.

PURURAVAS COULD NOT BELIEVE HIS EARS.

AT LAST SOMEONE HAS UNDERSTOOD MY PLIGHT. BUT WHO COULD IT BE?

AS HE LIFTED HIS EYES, HE SAW BEFORE HIM A FLOWERLESS, FORLORN CREEPER.

AH! POOR WAN CREEPER. YOU REMIND ME OF MY URVASHI.

NO SOONER HAD PURURAVAS ENCIRCLED THE CREEPER WITH HIS HANDS THAN—

WHAT TRICK IS THIS? I FEEL MY URVASHI'S ARMS. NO! I DARE NOT OPEN MY EYES AND FACE THE TRUTH.

INDEED, THE CREEPER WAS URVASHI.

MY LORD! OPEN YOUR EYES! PLEASE!

URVASHI! YOU! WHERE DID YOU GO? HOW COULD YOU HAVE TREATED ME SO?

URVASHI WAS ABOUT TO SAY SOMETHING WHEN SHE SAW THE JEWEL.

THE JEWEL OF REUNION! NOW I KNOW HOW I REGAINED MY FORM AS SOON AS YOU EMBRACED ME!

SHE EXPLAINED IT ALL TO A BEWILDERED PURURAVAS. THEN—

COME LET US RETURN TO YOUR PALACE. YOU HAVE BEEN AWAY A LONG TIME. PEOPLE WILL BLAME ME.

ABSENT FOR LONG, THE KING RETURNED TO A JUBILANT WELCOME IN THE CITY.

WHAT A WELCOME! THE KING HAS AT LAST RETURNED. EVERYONE IS HAPPY.

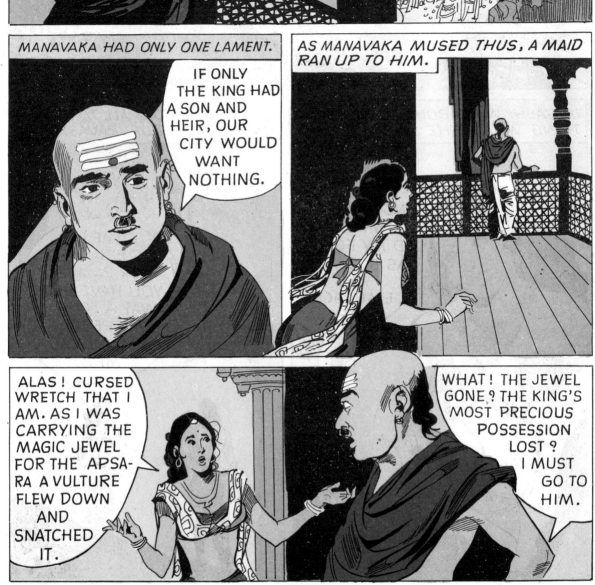

MANAVAKA HAD ONLY ONE LAMENT.

IF ONLY THE KING HAD A SON AND HEIR, OUR CITY WOULD WANT NOTHING.

AS MANAVAKA MUSED THUS, A MAID RAN UP TO HIM.

ALAS! CURSED WRETCH THAT I AM. AS I WAS CARRYING THE MAGIC JEWEL FOR THE APSA-RA A VULTURE FLEW DOWN AND SNATCHED IT.

WHAT! THE JEWEL GONE? THE KING'S MOST PRECIOUS POSSESSION LOST? I MUST GO TO HIM.

MANAVAKA RAN UP TO PURURAVAS.

THERE FLIES THE THIEF. WHY DON'T YOU SHOOT HIM DOWN?

I CANNOT. HE IS OUT OF REACH OF MY ARROW.

PURURAVAS CALLED HIS CHAMBERLAIN TO HIM.

THE THIEF MUST RETURN TO HIS NEST IN THE EVENING. TRACK HIM DOWN.

IT SHALL BE DONE, SIR.

AND THE CHAMBERLAIN LEFT.

BUT HE SOON RETURNED.

SEE WHAT I HAVE HERE. THE BIRD WAS SHOT DEAD BY THIS ARROW AND I HAVE RETRIEVED THE JEWEL.

WHOSE ARROW IS IT?

THE OWNER'S NAME IS CARVED HERE. BUT MY EYES ARE FEEBLE. I CAN'T READ IT.

WONDER OF WONDERS! THIS ARROW WAS SHOT BY AYUS THE SON OF URVASHI AND PURURAVAS.

MY FRIEND, A SON! WHAT MORE DO YOU WANT?

BUT THIS IS IMPOSSIBLE. I HAVE NOT BEEN SEPARATED FROM MY URVASHI FOR A SINGLE DAY EXCEPT WHEN SHE ENTERED KARTIKEYA'S GROVE. HOW COULD SHE HAVE HAD A SON I DIDN'T KNOW OF?

JUST THEN THE CHAMBERLAIN RE-ENTERED.

SIR, SATYAVATI, A HERMITESS FROM SAGE CHYAVANA'S ASHRAM WOULD LIKE TO SEE YOU. SHE HAS A BOY WITH HER.

BRING THEM IN AT ONCE.

AS THEY ENTERED—

WHY, HE IS A REPLICA OF YOU! HE MUST BE THE BOY WHO SHOT THE ARROW— YOUR SON.

HE MUST BE. HOW I LONG TO HOLD HIM IN MY ARMS.

SATYAVATI TOOK LEAVE OF PURURAVAS AND URVASHI AND WAS ABOUT TO GO WHEN—

MOTHER, TAKE ME WITH YOU.

I CAN'T, MY SON. YOU MUST NOW LIVE WITH YOUR FATHER AND REIGN AFTER HIM.

I WILL, MY SON. PEACE BE WITH ALL OF YOU.

THEN MOTHER, WILL YOU SEND MY PET PEACOCK TO ME?

WHEN SATYAVATI LEFT —

WHY, WHAT'S THE MATTER? THIS IS THE HAPPIEST DAY OF MY LIFE AND YOU GRIEVE.

I HAD FORGOTTEN MY-SELF IN A MOTHER'S JOY...

THEN URVASHI TOLD PURURAVAS ABOUT THE CONDITION LAID DOWN BY INDRA.

... NOW I WILL HAVE TO GO BACK. THIS IS MY LAST HOUR WITH YOU.

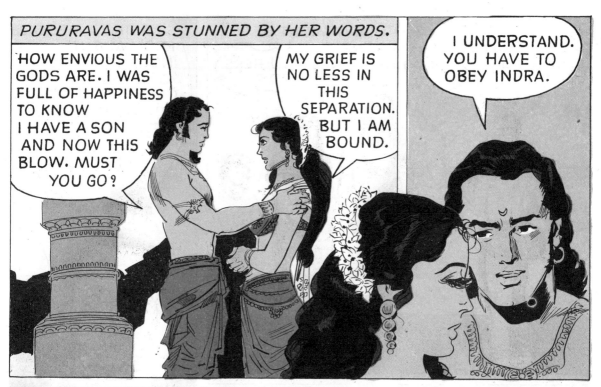

PURURAVAS WAS STUNNED BY HER WORDS.

HOW ENVIOUS THE GODS ARE. I WAS FULL OF HAPPINESS TO KNOW I HAVE A SON AND NOW THIS BLOW. MUST YOU GO?

MY GRIEF IS NO LESS IN THIS SEPARATION. BUT I AM BOUND.

I UNDERSTAND. YOU HAVE TO OBEY INDRA.

AS FOR ME, I SHALL CROWN AYUS KING, AND RETIRE TO THE FOREST.

JUST THEN A SUDDEN FLASH LIT THE SKY AND NARADA DESCENDED TO EARTH.

GREETINGS, LORD NARADA.

HAIL PURURAVAS, GREAT GUARDIAN OF THE EARTH!

MY RESPECTS, LORD.

31

MAY YOU TWO LIVE FOREVER IN CONJUGAL BLISS.

OH! THAT IT MIGHT BE SO. WHAT BRINGS YOU HERE, MY LORD?

I BRING A MESSAGE FROM MIGHTY INDRA. HE NEEDS YOUR HELP AGAINST THE ASURAS. HE DOES NOT WANT YOU TO RETIRE TO THE WOODS. HE HAS GIFTED URVASHI TO YOU FOR LIFE.

WHEN PURURAVAS AND URVASHI HEARD THIS—

IN ALL I AM INDRA'S GRATEFUL SERVANT.

THE PANGS IN MY HEART ARE STILLED FOREVER.

NARADA RETURNED TO THE HEAVENS. PURURAVAS LIVED HAPPILY WITH URVASHI TILL THE END OF HIS DAYS.

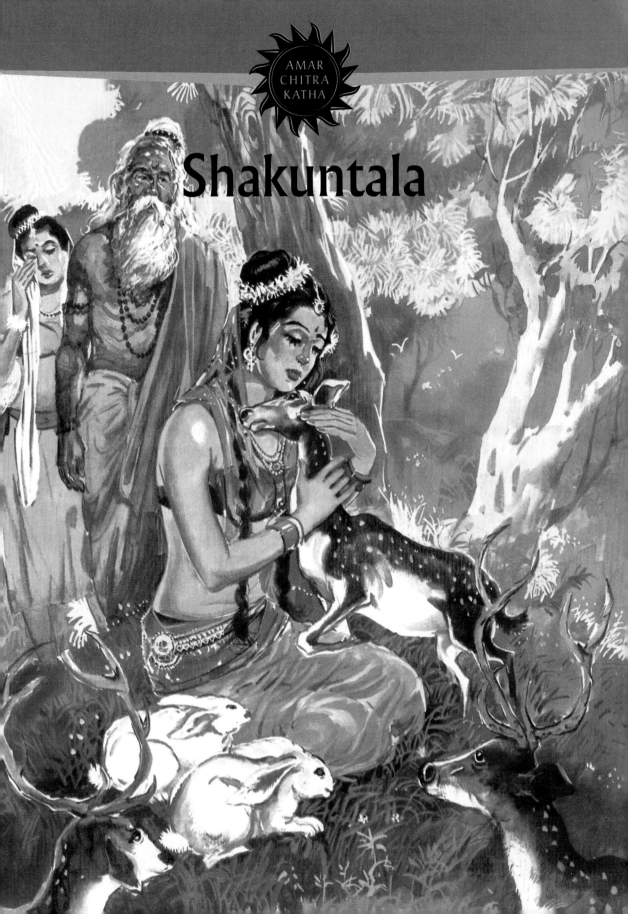

Illustrated Classics From India

# Shakuntala

The story of Shakuntala originally appeared in the first book of the Mahabharata where the lineage of the chief characters is detailed. It was later adapted with minor changes into a play by Kalidasa, the great Sanskrit poet and dramatist.

Shakuntala was the daughter of Sage Vishwamitra and Menaka, a celestial maiden. When Shakuntala was born, Menaka abandoned her near Sage Kanva's hermitage where he found her and made her his foster daughter. One day King Dushyanta of Hastinapura met her while he was hunting in the forest. Enamoured by her beauty, he married her and returned to his palace, promising to send for her at the soonest. Later, when Shakuntala went to his court, Dushyanta did not recognise her, owing to a curse placed on her by Sage Durvasa.

In the end, however, the truth of her claims was proved, and Shakuntala and Dushyanta were reunited. Their son Bharat, a direct ancestor of the Pandava and Kaurava princes, is the one who gave our country its name – 'Bharat'.

**Script: Dolat H. Doongaji and A.K. Lavangia    Illustrations: K.P. Shankar**

# SHAKUNTALA

MENAKA, A HEAVENLY NYMPH, LEFT HER NEW-BORN BABY NEAR SAGE KANVA'S HERMITAGE.

SHAKUNTAL BIRDS FLUTTERED ABOVE THE BABY. THE NOISE DISTURBED THE SAGE'S PRAYERS. HE LOOKED BEHIND AND SAW THE BABY.

THE SAGE PICKED IT UP.

I SHALL ADOPT THE BABY-GIRL AND CALL HER SHAKUNTALA.

THE BABY GREW UP AND MADE FRIENDS WITH THE ANIMALS AROUND HER.

SHAKUNTALA, NOW A BEAUTIFUL WOMAN, LED A USEFUL LIFE WITH HER FRIENDS PRIYAMVADA AND ANASUYA.

PRIYAMVADA, YOU ARE ALWAYS TEASING ANASUYA.

YOU ARE ALWAYS BUSY SHAKUNTALA, LET US HAVE SOME FUN.

ONE DAY, YOUNG KING DUSHYANT OF HASTINAPUR, CAME TO THAT FOREST TO HUNT.

LOOK! THERE IS A FINE STAG JUST AHEAD OF US.

WE WILL GO LIKE THE WIND AND HUNT IT DOWN.

I SHALL HUNT NO MORE, BUT GO FOR THE BLESSING OF THE SAGE.

STOP! THE FAWN BELONGS TO SAGE KANVA.

TAKE MY ROBES AND ORNAMENTS. I WILL GO IN SIMPLE CLOTHES AND MEET THE SAGE.

WHEN THE KING HEARD VOICES, HE HID BEHIND A TREE.

OH PRIYA, HELP ME! THERE IS A BEE WORRYING ME.

LUCKY BEE! TO TOUCH HER LOVELY FACE.

CALL THE KING TO HELP YOU, SHAKUNTALA. IT IS HIS DUTY TO HELP HIS SUBJECTS.

THE RING HAD THE KING'S SEAL ON IT.

OH! OUR GUEST IS THE KING HIMSELF.

WE ARE HONOURED BY YOUR VISIT.

LET US GO AND GET SOME FRUIT AND HONEY FOR THE KING.

OH! HOW BEAUTIFUL SHE IS!

WHAT A HANDSOME MAN HE IS!

PARDON US, SIR, WE HAVE VERY SIMPLE FOOD TO OFFER YOU.

PLEASE SIT DOWN AND HAVE SOME FRUIT WITH US.

WHILE THE KING WAS EATING, SOME HERMITS CAME ALONG.

WON'T YOU PROTECT US FROM THE DEMONS OF THIS FOREST? THEY DISTURB OUR PRAYERS.

DON'T WORRY, I SHALL REMAIN HERE TILL I DESTROY ALL THE DEMONS.

WE SHALL ALWAYS BE GRATEFUL TO YOU.

AFTER SOME DAYS WHEN THE KING WAS KEEPING WATCH FOR THE DEMONS, HE HEARD VOICES.

LET ME HIDE HERE AND LISTEN.

TELL US WHY YOU LOOK SO SAD, DEAR SHAKUNTALA.

HOW BRAVE AND GOOD OUR KING IS. I WISH I COULD MARRY A MAN LIKE HIM. BUT I AM ONLY A POOR VILLAGE GIRL.

SINCE YOU ARE SO SHY, WHY DON'T YOU WRITE TO HIM? HERE IS A LOTUS LEAF. WRITE ON IT WITH YOUR NAIL.

I do not know what you think of me, but I think you are the most wonderful man on earth

I MUST TAKE THIS LETTER TO THE KING.

GAUTAMI, AN OLD LADY, WAS LIKE A MOTHER TO SHAKUNTALA. SHE MADE PREPARATIONS FOR SHAKUNTALA TO LEAVE.

OUR SHAKUNTALA DOES NOT HAVE CLOTHES AND JEWELS FIT FOR A BRIDE.

THE GODS ALWAYS HELP THE GOOD.

SUDDENLY A MIRACLE HAPPENED.

OH LOOK! WHAT LOVELY CLOTHES ARE HERE!

ON EVERY BRANCH THERE'S A SHINING JEWEL.

OH SHAKUNTALA, HOW LOVELY YOU LOOK IN THESE CLOTHES.

NOW THAT YOU WILL BE LIVING IN A PALACE, YOU WILL FORGET YOUR POOR FRIENDS.

I WILL NEVER FORGET YOU. I WILL COME TO MEET YOU OFTEN.

SAD AT PARTING, THE PLANT CLUNG TO HER. TAKE CARE OF MY FAWN AND ALL MY OTHER PETS.

OH CREATURES OF THE FOREST! SAY GOOD-BYE TO SHAKUNTALA WHO ALWAYS LOVED AND CARED FOR YOU.

FATHER KANVA WAS ALSO SAD. THE TREES SHED TEARS IN THE FORM OF LEAVES. PEACOCKS STOPPED DANCING AND THE DEER FORGOT TO EAT.

A FEW DAYS LATER, A MESSENGER CAME.

YOUR MAJESTY, THERE IS URGENT WORK IN HASTINA-PUR AND YOU MUST LEAVE IMMEDIATELY.

I WILL COME AT ONCE.

I MUST GO NOW, DEAREST. WEAR THIS RING ON YOUR FINGER ALWAYS.

GOOD-BYE, SHAKUNTALA! I SHALL SOON SEND MY MINISTERS TO BRING YOU TO MY PALACE.

SOMETIME LATER, SAGE DURVASA PAID A VISIT TO THE HERMITAGE. SHAKUN-TALA WAS THINKING ABOUT HER HUSBAND.

WHERE'S MY FRIEND KANVA? DOES NO ONE WELCOME A GUEST IN THIS PLACE?

AFTER SOME WEEKS —

OH! WHEN WILL DUSHYANT SEND FOR ME?

IF ONLY FATHER KANVA WERE HERE, HE WOULD KNOW WHAT TO DO.

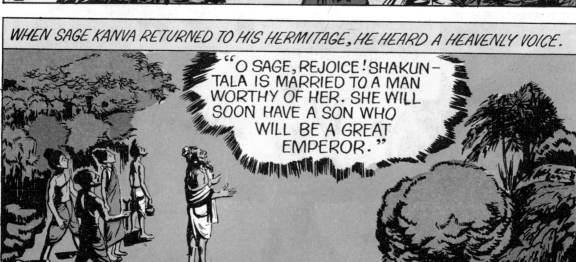

WHEN SAGE KANVA RETURNED TO HIS HERMITAGE, HE HEARD A HEAVENLY VOICE.

"O SAGE, REJOICE! SHAKUN-TALA IS MARRIED TO A MAN WORTHY OF HER. SHE WILL SOON HAVE A SON WHO WILL BE A GREAT EMPEROR."

THE SAGE WAS WELCOMED BY THE GIRLS.

I HAVE HEARD THE GOOD NEWS. NOW WE MUST SEND YOU TO YOUR HUSBAND.

SUDDENLY THERE WAS A BRIGHT LIGHT IN THE SKY. SHAKUNTALA'S MOTHER APPEARED.

WHO IS THIS HEAVENLY NYMPH?

THE NYMPH CARRIED AWAY SHAKUNTALA INTO THE CLOUDS.

THIS IS VERY STRANGE! I MUST TELL THE KING ABOUT IT.

A FEW DAYS LATER A FISHERMAN WAS ARRESTED IN THE BAZAAR.

LET ME GO! I DID NOT STEAL THIS RING.

YOU THIEF! IT IS THE KING'S RING. IT HAS HIS SEAL ON IT.

DURVASA'S CURSE HAD WORKED. THE KING HAD FORGOTTEN SHAKUNTALA.

I WONDER WHAT THEY WANT WITH ME. SHOW THEM IN.

YOUR MAJESTY, SOME INMATES OF SAGE KANVA'S ASHRAM HAVE COME TO SEE YOU.

SAGE KANVA GREETS YOU AND HAS SENT SHAKUNTALA, YOUR WIFE, WHO WILL SOON BE A MOTHER.

THE KING LOOKED SURPRISED.

DON'T YOU REMEMBER YOUR WIFE, SHAKUNTALA?

THE RING MUST HAVE FALLEN SOMEWHERE. LET US LOOK FOR IT.

I DON'T KNOW WHAT YOU ARE TALKING ABOUT.

SHAKUNTALA, RAISE YOUR VEIL. THE KING WILL SURELY REMEMBER YOU WHEN HE SEES YOUR FACE.

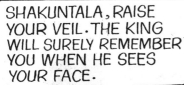

YOUR FACE IS INDEED LOVELY BUT I HAVE NEVER SEEN YOU BEFORE.

DO YOU REMEMBER HOW ONE DAY YOU COLLECTED RAIN-WATER IN A LOTUS FLOWER AND GAVE IT TO MY PET FAWN TO DRINK BUT SHE REFUSED.

YET WHEN I OFFERED IT, SHE DRANK IT GLADLY. SO YOU SAID — YOU ARE BOTH CHILDREN OF THE FOREST AND TRUST EACH OTHER... AND...

STOP YOUR CHATTER. I REMEMBER NO SUCH THING.

OH DUSHYANT! IT IS WICKED OF YOU TO DISOWN YOUR OWN WIFE.

THE KING WAS VERY SAD.

OH SHAKUNTALA! HOW CRUELLY I HAVE TREATED YOU. HOW COULD I FORGET YOU?

CALL THE CHIEF PRIEST.

WHERE IS MY WIFE SHAKUNTALA? WHO WILL BRING MY BELOVED BACK TO ME?

A NYMPH CARRIED HER AWAY AND SHE IS LOST FOR EVER.

HERE IS LOVELY SHAKUNTALA IN THE GARDEN. HERE IS HER JASMINE CREEPER AND THERE IS HER PET FAWN...

FOR A FEW YEARS THE KING LED A QUIET LIFE THINKING OF SHAKUNTALA ALL THE TIME. ONE DAY—

GOD INDRA HAS SENT MATALI WITH A MESSAGE.

SHOW HIM IN.

THE GODS WANT YOUR HELP IN A WAR AGAINST THE DEMONS.

I AM READY TO HELP.

A TERRIBLE WAR WAS FOUGHT BETWEEN THE DEMONS AND THE GODS.

THE GODS WON THE WAR AND DUSHYANT CAME BACK TO EARTH IN MATALI'S FLYING CHARIOT.

WHAT LOVELY SCENERY! HOW HAPPY THE CREATURES OF THE EARTH LOOK. I ALONE AM UNHAPPY.

GOOD-BYE DUSHYANT! MAY THE GODS REWARD YOU FOR YOUR BRAVERY.

WHERE AM I? THIS IS A STRANGE PLACE WHICH I HAVE NEVER SEEN BEFORE.

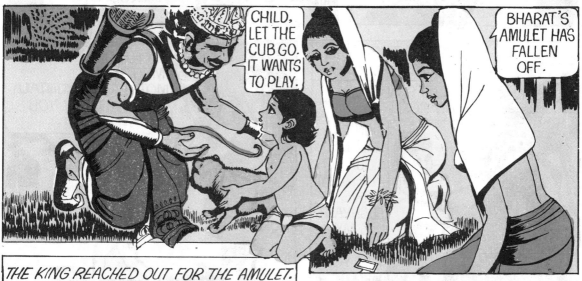

IT IS A MAGIC AMULET GIVEN BY SAGE MARICHA. IT WAS TIED ROUND THE CHILD'S ARM TO KEEP HIM FROM HARM. ONLY HIS PARENTS CAN TOUCH IT.

WHAT HAPPENS IF SOME ONE ELSE TOUCHES IT?

IT TURNS INTO A SNAKE AND BITES THAT PERSON.

THE KING RUSHED TO THE CHILD AND PICKED HIM UP.

OH, MY SON! MY SON!

DON'T CALL ME YOUR SON. THE GREAT KING DUSHYANT IS MY FATHER, NOT YOU.

LITTLE ONE, TAKE ME TO YOUR MOTHER, SHAKUNTALA. SHE WILL TELL YOU WHO I AM.

MOTHER, HERE'S A MAN WHO KEEPS CALLING ME HIS SON. HE WANTS TO SEE YOU.

OH DUSHYANT, SO YOU HAVE COME AT LAST.

# Malavika

An Adaptation of Kalidasa's
Sanskrit Play "Malavikagnimitra"

Illustrated Classics From India

# Malavika
### An Adaptation of Kalidasa's Sanskrit Play, Malavikagnimitra

The story Malavika is based on poet-writer Kalidasa's play *Malavikagnimitra*. Kalidasa is respected as one of the greatest poets and playwrights of all time. Scholars are not quite certain about the time and date in which Kalidasa lived and wrote. From the 6th century BC to the 10th century AD, various dates are proved and disproved to be the period in which Kalidasa lived. But when it comes to Kalidasa's writings, there are no two opinions - they are unanimously considered exquisite.

As Kalidasa's first play, *Malavikagnimitra* has more of the young enthusiastic writer's sense of fun, play and intrigue than the spectacular imagery and poetic expressions displayed in his later works. Kalidasa was a court poet and the play reveals his first grand experience of the intrigue and cunning, and the jealousy, love and valour that rage behind royal curtains.

The poet's more memorable works are *Abhijnana-Shakuntalam, Ritusamhara, Raghuvamsha, Kumarasambhava, Vikramorvashiya* and the famous *Meghduta*, which is a matchless work of poetry. Kalidasa is respected all over the world as one of the greatest poets and playwrights. Some of his works have been translated into almost all the major languages of the world.

**Script: Kamlesh Pandey     Illustrations: P.B. Kavadi**

# MALAVIKA

DURING THE SECOND CENTURY B.C. THE TWO COUSINS, YAJNASENA AND MADHAVA-SENA WERE ENGAGED IN A STRUGGLE FOR THE THRONE OF VIDARBHA. ONE DAY, AT DUSK, TWO CHARIOTS STOLE AWAY FROM VIDARBHA AND TOOK THE ROAD TO VIDISHA, A NEIGHBOURING KINGDOM RULED BY AGNIMITRA. ONE OF THE CHARIOTS CARRIED PRINCE MADHAVASENA; PRINCESS MALAVIKA, HIS SISTER; SUMATI, HIS MINISTER AND KAUSHIKI SUMATI'S SISTER; THE OTHER, THEIR ATTENDANTS.

1

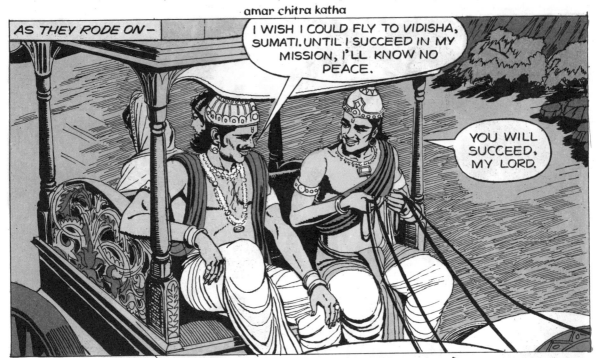

AS THEY RODE ON —

I WISH I COULD FLY TO VIDISHA, SUMATI. UNTIL I SUCCEED IN MY MISSION, I'LL KNOW NO PEACE.

YOU WILL SUCCEED, MY LORD.

I WONDER WHAT KIND OF CITY VIDISHA IS, KAUSHIKI.

YOU'LL SEE FOR YOURSELF WHEN WE REACH THERE, MALAVIKA.

A LITTLE LATER, AS THEY TURNED A BEND IN THE ROAD, MADHAVASENA SUDDENLY STARTED.

SUMATI, DO YOU SEE THOSE MEN THERE?

I DO. THEY'RE SOLDIERS.

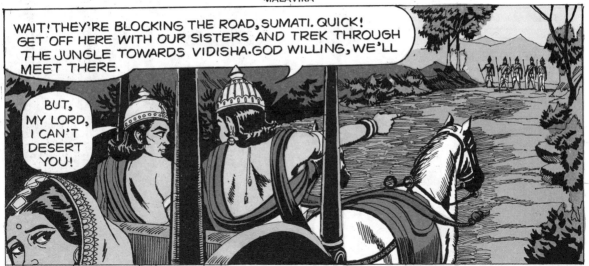

A FEW MINUTES LATER —

WELCOME, MADHAVA-SENA. YAJNASENA, THE KING OF VIDARBHA, INVITES YOU TO BE HIS HONOURED GUEST...

...AT HIS PRISON CELL.

AND THE SOLDIERS MARCHED AWAY WITH MADHAVASENA, HIS CHARIOTS AND HIS ATTENDANTS.

COME, MY CHILD. I SEE A CARAVAN MOVING TOWARDS VIDISHA. WE'LL JOIN THEM.

CONTROLLING THEIR EMOTIONS, THE THREE TREKKED WITH THE CARAVAN.

WHEN NIGHT FELL —

WE'LL HALT NOW, MY FRIEND. WE'LL MOVE ON AGAIN TOMORROW MORNING.

SUMATI, KAUSHIKI AND MALAVIKA TRIED TO RELAX BUT THEIR HEARTS WERE HEAVY.

WHAT DOES FATE HAVE IN STORE FOR ME?

I CANNOT REST TILL I REACH VIDISHA AND FULFIL MY PROMISE.

SUDDENLY —

WHAT IS THIS? WHERE DID IT COME FROM?

AHHH!!

ROBBERS! RUN FOR YOUR LIVES!

WAIT! DON'T RUN AWAY! LET'S FIGHT THEM.

GO, HIDE SOMEWHERE. AS LONG AS I'M ALIVE, NOTHING WILL HAPPEN TO EITHER OF YOU. I'LL FIGHT THEM SINGLE-HANDED, IF NECESSARY.

SUMATI PUT UP A BRAVE FIGHT.

AHHH!

A FEW OTHERS FROM THE CARAVAN JOINED HIM BUT THE ROBBERS PROVED TO BE STRONGER.

LET'S FLEE! WE CAN'T MATCH THEM!

WHEN THE JUBILANT ROBBERS LEFT WITH THEIR BOOTY, KAUSHIKI CAME OUT FROM BEHIND SOME BUSHES.

NO! SUMATI, MY DEAR, DEAR BROTHER! SPEAK TO ME. ALAS! WHAT WILL I DO NOW? POOR MALAVIKA···

8

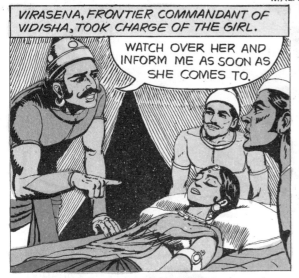

VIRASENA, FRONTIER COMMANDANT OF VIDISHA, TOOK CHARGE OF THE GIRL.

WATCH OVER HER AND INFORM ME AS SOON AS SHE COMES TO.

A LITTLE LATER —

SIR, SHE'S OPENED HER EYES!

WHO ARE YOU, GENTLE MAIDEN? WHERE DO YOU···

MY NAME IS MALAVIKA. PLEASE DO NOT ASK ME ANYTHING ELSE.

AS YOU WISH. I WILL TAKE YOU TO OUR QUEEN. YOU WILL BE SAFE WITH HER.

VIRASENA TOOK MALAVIKA TO DHARINI, AGNIMITRA'S CHIEF QUEEN.

IT'S GOOD THAT YOU BROUGHT HER HERE, VIRASENA. SHE SHALL BE MY OWN MAID. I'LL SEND HER TO GANA-DASA TO LEARN DANCING.

THUS THE TURN DESTINY TOOK FINALLY LANDED MALAVIKA IN THE PALACE AT VIDISHA. HER DESTINATION, BUT IN A ROLE SHE HAD NEVER DREAMT OF.

A FEW DAYS LATER—

A FEMALE MENDICANT WISHES TO SEE HER MAJESTY. MAY I BRING HER IN?

LEAD THE REVERED ONE IN.

AS SOON AS KAUSHIKI ENTERED—

MALAVIKA! HERE! OH, HOW RELIEVED I AM! BUT I MUST NOT DISCLOSE HER IDENTITY. I MUST WAIT FOR THE RIGHT MOMENT.

IT'S KAUSHIKI! DISGUISED AS A MENDICANT!

I'M HONOURED TO HAVE YOU WITH US, PARIVRAJIKA.*

MAY GOD BLESS YOU, NOBLE QUEEN.

AS DHARINI TURNED TO GIVE THE MAID ORDERS...

...KAUSHIKI AND MALAVIKA MADE A SILENT PACT.

* A FEMALE MENDICANT

10

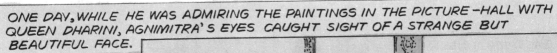

ONE DAY, WHILE HE WAS ADMIRING THE PAINTINGS IN THE PICTURE-HALL WITH QUEEN DHARINI, AGNIMITRA'S EYES CAUGHT SIGHT OF A STRANGE BUT BEAUTIFUL FACE.

WHO IS THIS GIRL, MY QUEEN? I'VE NEVER SEEN HER BEFORE.

JUST ONE OF MY MAIDS.

WHAT'S HER NAME?

I DON'T KNOW!

DHARINI'S YOUNG SISTER VASULAXMI, ANSWERED HIS QUESTION

I KNOW! I KNOW! IT'S MALAVIKA.

THE NAME STUCK IN HIS MEMORY. AND SO DID THE FACE. THAT NIGHT AGNIMITRA COULDN'T SLEEP.

MALAVIKA. WHAT A BEAUTIFUL NAME! WHAT A FACE···! I MUST SEE HER IN PERSON.

THE NEXT DAY, HE SENT FOR GAUTAMA, HIS VIDUSHAKA.*

GAUTAMA, I NEED YOUR HELP. I SAW MALAVIKA'S PORTRAIT, ACCIDENTALLY, AND NOW, I CRAVE TO SEE HER.

THAT'S EASILY DONE, MY LORD.

BUT HOW?

YOU ARE CLEVER INDEED, GAUTAMA!

WELL, MAY I TAKE YOUR LEAVE NOW? THERE'S WORK TO BE DONE.

* KING'S JESTER.

GAUTAMA FIRST WENT TO GANADASA.

DO YOU KNOW WHAT HARADATTA, YOUR RIVAL, HAS BEEN SAYING ABOUT YOU AT COURT? HE SAYS, 'AS A DANCE-TEACHER, GANADASA IS NOT EQUAL EVEN TO THE DUST OF MY FEET.'

DID HE SAY THAT? I MUST COMPLAIN TO HIS MAJESTY. I WILL NOT TOLERATE THIS INSULT. I WILL GO RIGHT NOW.

LATER, AT HARADATTA'S HOUSE —

I SHOULDN'T MENTION THIS BUT SINCE I'M YOUR WELL-WISHER, I CAN'T HELP IT. GANADASA HAS BEEN SAYING THAT THE DIFFERENCE BE-TWEEN HIM AND YOU IS AS GREAT AS BETWEEN THE OCEAN AND A PUDDLE.

I WILL SHOW THAT 'OCEAN' WHAT A 'PUDDLE' I AM. I'M GOING TO HIS MAJESTY RIGHT AWAY.

AT AGNIMITRA'S PALACE —

JUSTICE, YOUR MAJESTY! I HAVE BEEN INSULTED BY THIS HARADATTA.

HE BEGAN IT, YOUR MAJESTY! LET THERE BE A FAIR TRIAL OF OUR TALENTS, AND THE MATTER BE SETTLED.

PEACE, MY GOOD MEN! THE TRIAL SHALL BE HELD.

A CONTEST WAS ARRANGED. KAUSHIKI WAS SELECTED TO JUDGE THE PERFORMANCES. GANADASA'S PUPIL, MALAVIKA, WAS THE FIRST TO PERFORM.

MY BELOVED IS HERE. YET HOW CAN I APPROACH HIM? WHAT A HOPELESS LOVE IS MINE!

KNOW, MY BELOVED, THAT I YEARN FOR YOU.

THE WORDS OF THE SONG EXPRESSED MALAVIKA'S OWN FEELINGS.

I, TOO, YEARN FOR YOU, MALAVIKA.

14

WHEN THE PERFORMANCE CAME TO AN END —

IT WAS PERFECT!

CONGRATULATIONS, GANADASA!

IT'S MEALTIME NOW. SHOULDN'T WE POSTPONE HARADATTA'S TURN FOR TOMORROW?

YOU ARE RIGHT, GAUTAMA.

WHAT DO YOU SAY, HARADATTA?

AS YOU WISH, YOUR MAJESTY.

NOW WHAT, GAUTAMA? I'M MORE RESTLESS THAN EVER...

FIRST LET ME EAT.

I CAN'T WAIT TO MEET HER, MY FRIEND.

PATIENCE, MY LORD, YOU SHALL... VERY SOON.

A FEW DAYS LATER, THE PALACE GARDENS RESOUNDED WITH LAUGHTER AS THE WOMEN OF THE ROYAL HOUSEHOLD, BATHED IN THE FRAGRANCE OF FRESH BLOSSOMS, CELEBRATED THE SPRING FESTIVAL.

DHARINI TOO WAS THERE, WITH MALAVIKA ATTENDING ON HER. SUDDENLY, GAUTAMA CAME UPON THE SCENE.

LET ME PUSH OUR NOBLE QUEEN FOR A WHILE, MALAVIKA.

HELP! I'M SLIPPING!

DHARINI LANDED WITH A THUD.

O GAUTAMA, HOW CARE-LESS OF YOU! I'VE TWISTED MY ANKLE!

I'M SORRY, YOUR MAJESTY !···!···

JUST AS I EXPECTED.

ENOUGH, ENOUGH! NOW I WILL NOT BE ABLE TO FUL-FIL THE LONGING OF THE GOLDEN ASHOKA* MALAVIKA, YOU TRY. IF THE ASHOKA BLOSSOMS WITHIN FIVE DAYS, I'LL GRANT YOU A BOON.

*A TREE WHICH WOULD BLOSSOM ONLY IF A BEAUTIFUL WOMAN STRUCK IT WITH A DECORATED FOOT.

MEANWHILE, IRAVATI, AGNIMITRA'S SECOND WIFE, SENT HIM A GIFT OF RED ASHOKA BLOSSOMS ALONG WITH AN INVITATION

I WISH TO ENJOY MY LORD'S COMPANY ON THE SWING.

ACCEPT IT, YOUR MAJESTY. IT SUITS MY PLAN.

IN AGNIMITRA'S PALACE GARDEN —

HERE WE ARE, FRIEND. LOOK! SPRING HAS TOUCHED EVERYTHING. NOW WHERE IS HER LADYSHIP?

PATIENCE, YOUR MAJESTY. BAKULAVALIKA, THE MAID, HAS PROMISED TO DO HER BEST.

AH! THERE SHE IS! OH, MALAVIKA!

HUSH, YOUR MAJESTY. LET US CREEP BEHIND THAT BUSH AND WATCH HER.

IN THE CELLAR —

NOW WHAT, BAKULA? WILL WE HAVE TO SPEND THE REST OF OUR LIVES HERE?

NO, MY FRIEND. IF I KNOW THE VIDUSHAKA, WE'LL SOON BE OUT. AND YOU'LL BE SPENDING THE REST OF YOUR LIFE WITH THE KING.

BAKULAVALIKA WAS RIGHT. THE KING WAS VISITING THE INJURED DHARINI WHEN —

HELP! HELP! I'VE BEEN BITTEN BY A SNAKE.

I HAD GONE TO PICK FLOWERS FOR THE QUEEN WHEN IT BIT ME. AH! I'M DYING...PLEASE LOOK AFTER MY AGED MOTHER...

ALAS! I'VE BECOME THE CAUSE OF HIS DEATH!

THE VAID!* WILL SOMEONE TAKE HIM TO THE VAID?

GOOD BYE, YOUR LADYSHIP.

*PHYSICIAN

GAUTAMA WAS CARRIED AWAY. A LITTLE LATER—

VICTORY TO THE KING! THE VAID NEEDS SOMETHING HAVING THE IMAGE OF A SNAKE.

HERE, TAKE MY RING WITH THE SERPENT-SEAL. BUT RETURN IT TO ME AND NONE ELSE.

WITHIN MOMENTS, GAUTAMA, WHO WAS ONLY PRETENDING, WAS AT THE DOOR OF THE TREASURE-CELLAR WITH THE RING.

THE KING HAS ORDERED THE RELEASE OF THE PRISONERS, MALAVIKA AND BAKULAVALIKA. HERE'S THE QUEEN'S RING.

LATER IN THE GARDEN—

YOU TWO WAIT HERE. I'M GOING TO BRING THE KING.

YOUR MAJESTY, COME WITH ME, QUICK!

AS SOON AS AGNIMITRA SAW MALAVIKA—

COME, COME TO ME, DEAR ONE.

BUT THE QUEEN! I'M AFRAID OF THE QUEEN.

FEAR NOT, DEAR ONE. FEAR NOT.

I SAW THE BRAVE KING IN VERY MUCH THE SAME STATE AS I AM— BEFORE THE QUEEN.

SUDDENLY—

I'M SORRY IF I'VE DISTURBED YOU.

SHE ONLY CAME TO THANK ME FOR RELEASING HER.

24

BEFORE IRAVATI COULD SAY ANOTHER WORD—

YOUR MAJESTY, YOUR MAJESTY, PRINCESS VASULAXMI IS UNCONSCIOUS. SHE WAS FRIGHTENED BY A MONKEY.

I MUST RUSH TO HER.

MALAVIKA AND BAKULA WERE LEFT ALONE.

WHAT NOW! WHEN I THINK OF THE QUEEN, I TREMBLE.

TAKE HEART, MALAVIKA. LOOK! THE ASHOKA HAS BURST INTO BLOOM.

EVEN BEFORE THE LAPSE OF FIVE NIGHTS!

AND THE QUEEN IS ONE WHO KEEPS A PROMISE, MALAVIKA!

WHEN DHARINI HEARD THE GOOD NEWS—

REQUEST MY LORD TO MEET ME BY THE FLOWERING TREE. TOGETHER WE SHALL WITNESS THE SPLENDOUR OF THE BLOSSOMS.

AS AGNIMITRA AND GAUTAMA WAITED BY THE TREE FOR DHARINI—

SO, EVEN THE GOLDEN ASHOKA HAS BLOSSOMED. WILL THE SPRING LEAVE ONLY MY LOVE UNFULFILLED?

NOT FOR MUCH LONGER, MY LORD. LOOK THERE!

AND WHEN AGNIMITRA LOOKED, HE COULDN'T BELIEVE HIS EYES.

MALAVIKA IN BRIDAL FINERY! I WONDER WHAT THE QUEEN'S INTENTIONS ARE?

I KNOW WHY THE QUEEN HAS BROUGHT ME HERE DECKED OUT AS A BRIDE. YET I AM NERVOUS.

JUST AS DHARINI TURNED TO TAKE ONE LAST LOOK AT MALAVIKA BEFORE ADDRESSING THE KING···

···A MESSENGER BURST UPON THE SCENE. A GREAT DEAL HAD HAPPENED AT VIDISHA'S FRONTIER. KING YAJNASENA HAD BEEN DEFEATED AND MADHAVASENA LIBERATED.

TWO MAIDS PRESENTED BY THE NEW KING OF VIDARBHA AWAIT YOUR MAJESTY'S PLEASURE.

YOU MAY SEND THEM TO ME.

WHEN THE MAIDS CAME—

VICTORY TO THE KING! VICTORY TO THE QUEEN!

AND WHAT MAY YOUR SPECIAL TALENTS BE?

LORD! WE ARE WELL-VERSED IN MUSIC.

MY QUEEN, TAKE ANY ONE OF THESE TWO.

MALAVIKA, WHICH ONE WOULD YOU LIKE?

THE NAME SURPRISED THE MAIDS AS MUCH AS THEIR REACTION SURPRISED AGNIMITRA.

OUR PRINCESS! ALIVE!

MALAVIKA! OH, PRINCESS! VICTORY TO THE PRINCESS.

HOW DO YOU KNOW MALAVIKA?

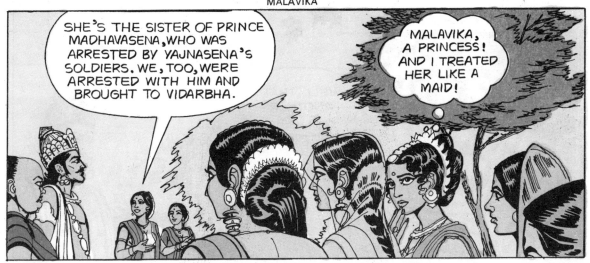

SHE'S THE SISTER OF PRINCE MADHAVASENA, WHO WAS ARRESTED BY YAJNASENA'S SOLDIERS. WE, TOO, WERE ARRESTED WITH HIM AND BROUGHT TO VIDARBHA.

MALAVIKA, A PRINCESS! AND I TREATED HER LIKE A MAID!

AND MALAVIKA? HOW DID SHE REACH HERE?

WE DO NOT KNOW, YOUR MAJESTY.

I KNOW! I'LL TELL YOU.

IT WAS KAUSHIKI.

THE NOBLE KAUSHIKI!

YES, THE MOMENT HAS COME TO TELL ALL. BEFORE MADHAVASENA WAS CAPTURED HE URGED SUMATI, MY BROTHER, TO FLEE WITH MALAVIKA, YOUR BETROTHED, AND ME, TO VIDISHA. ON THE WAY···

AS KAUSHIKI ENDED HER TALE—

WELL, THAT'S ANOTHER STORY.

BUT WHY DIDN'T YOU TELL US ALL THIS EARLIER?

WHEN MALAVIKA WAS A CHILD, IT WAS PROPHESIED THAT SHE WOULD GO THROUGH THE STATUS OF A SERVANT FOR ONE YEAR. THEN SHE WOULD MARRY A KING.

THAT'S WHY I KEPT THE SECRET FOR A WHOLE YEAR.

YOU DID WELL TO KEEP THE SECRET.

THEN SHE MUST MARRY A KING!

MY LORD, PLEASE ACCEPT MALAVIKA AS YOUR BRIDE.

AS YOU COMMAND, MY QUEEN.

THUS WERE AGNIMITRA AND MALAVIKA UNITED FOR EVER.